Frédéric Delalot

Another era

KDP Editions

The pleasures were mooring

And in Montreal, centuries had passed...

A logic illuminates the long cliffs...

Creatures, reason for seconds...

We were together, a few times...

Together, by June fever, unnoticed

And really, the time of the crowds

Ignoring routine, on the street...

Escapes from an illusion...

In how many worlds, facades...

Sheets at a distance...

The sap of ancient times...

Long necklaces, going up Sainte-Catherine

We drive back to the ports...

I remembered a speed, words

Yellow, walking under the sky...

Thrilling moment, at the post office...

By the way, Hindu tunes

Crossovers

Memories of trips, expectation of the anchor

Quick street tours...

Roads, panoramas...

So many moments...

In a cabin in height...

Some summer evenings, in the cellars

Ringing shores, impatience...

Time releases...

Behind translucent doors...

From place to daydreams, indefinable inspiration

Largesse, near the driveway

New times...

So, between two bays...

Illuminated ancestry of indirect projectors

The South, a febrile moment...

After seasons, appeasement...

Nostalgic, tourist compartment

We were loving America.

2

I order a coffee, literary salon, to wait

The bonds that united us were an ocean...

I was one of those who worked, on the surfaces of the service

They were a kind of planetary wandering, the idle project

Like deep memories, happiness...

Anachronistic, I wrote a date, next to a text

The pleasures were mooring

Nothing happens, everything remembers

Of a silence, in the corners ...

We are free...

Manhattan...

Eight thousand years separate us

I had time in front of me

Outside, a strange landscape, composition

In Montmartre, time was imaginary...

And in Montreal, centuries had passed...

The north wind would sweep the streets...

The large park was gradually overflowing into the city

Hotels and mezzanines, mirrors, Java bubbles...

The blank page was waiting for me, it was rushing...

Many fall asleep, life stretches...

Winding paths of Cap Nègre, the minutes were spread out

A web of words overwhelmed the city, in the center...

Remote fortifications, very far from hyperpoles...

That's it: everything happens, without errors, the mirror is right...

It was a memory, a future, twins...

The pride of the heights, with each wave...

A logic illuminates the long cliffs...

The steps are inner, the truth intact

Even the world of tomorrow

Looks a bit like the material

Vital momentum, after that moment

Initiating relaxation, blue plants

Frame, jousting, the leaves of a plant...

Fat, reached the ceiling, starry sky...

To the Sailing School, the pond of Pissevaches

Dark sea, copper, in Old Montreal.

3

Ah! the second hand of the large pools, red balconies

Leaves flew away in the nascent spring

The old places appeared, at the bottom of the screens

To judge the progress of a given society

Ecstatic stalemates, unspeakable trances...

Parks, seasons of remains, ancient steps

We are of an expansionist opinion, often...

Until we meet, the word is strong, our psyches...

The story we continued, Avenue du Levant...

The hood in a coastal fence...

Join the sidewalks, dandyism

Affable axes, underground

Victorious and complex passion...

While creating served to be free

Library, cafes, walks...

South American atmosphere, multitude...

From paintings to walls, perhaps enigma

A subtle reason languished

The Sun, during the day, played between the branches

In its pure state, taste of a sudden rhythm...

Areas far from the resorts, little by little...

I was thinking about stealth happiness...

In ancient times, we no longer age...

Ostentatious splendor of our feelings, confusing...

We passed the erubescent, ornate terraces

This strange mountain, glimpsed many times

Maybe love, maybe nothingness...

Who carried the luster of the shores, the evenings

Beyond comparisons, at the source...

The words, the word were unraveling

What can be said about the adventure?

Path, bare branches...

Near castles, with born desires

Along the arches

She was talking to me...

Pleasant flexibility...

Armchair, small tables.

4

Long periods, printing

The first moments of the stay

In the crowd, with a delight

Unparalleled, trends, paper...

Or swimming pools, in view of the city...

I was writing a date, next to a text

This arid hour must invent the paradigm...

One night, and a sea taxi would drop me off at your house

In the west, like those ostensible trips...

Producing, first, an irrepressible desire...

Of movement, smoother empires that we liked

From the new century, circumflex and transposable

It was a construction of the mind, a parade...

A lighthouse in the night, the gigantic lighthouse of the city

The Atlantic, a quarter moon, navigation, latitude...

I know that our analytical capabilities are looming...

Let's take it back: you like me, we knew how to reveal...

In a minimal way, reading books...

Always fluid, temporary distances...

Previous years, oceanic canvases

Tell anything, the thread of life...

The sequence of days, the drunkenness...

Myths of youth, joys listed

How many nights, how many days...

Bright orange, new century...

Aesthetic, I transmute, I'm sure...

I greet our youth, great marches

The trip offered us the cellars, the bars

The cafes and the alcove, almost late...

While placing them on the throne, invented...

So much desired, invisible splendor, punctuations

Blurred, festive air, meadows preserved, guarded ...

By our apogee, model, chapter, adoration

From the source, elegance...

Rub shoulders with secrets, ideas...

I contemplate the sun, remember

It was already writing the dream, like that.

Satiated, out of bounds

A century was going to melt...

In one dimension, something

All the same, nothing to upset

And the time of summers, winters

To snuggle up, how many ponds...

In how many worlds, facades

Perfect harmonies, that's the time

I envied you, my senseless nights.

Balafons of dreams...

Undressed, between sofas

Refined, far away, there...

For good, all...

What I believe...

Combining flows

Sheets at a distance...

Controls the valleys

I turn away, now...

We need to create something

New, a Hindu or Brazilian air

Interfered afternoon

Large streets, exterior stairs

At random smooth, perfect body...

She seemed to live in a world...

Sporty, years that slipped without a grip

At the end of the week, I was passing...

At the café, it was a different time

The sap of ancient times...

Remains of sleepless nights...

Planetary interests, and I was thinking about this parenthesis

From distracted anarchy, brewing, there is the clean way

Unitary, sieve of agitations, in this other space...

Temporal, without even worrying about it, art and speech...

Whole medals, singular revolt

Attempted wanderings, simplification

International code, all camouflaged...

Interior, volumes, up and down.

Did we forget the symphony?

A whisper launches the call...

Come to think of it, fantasy...

To be synchronized: we were going to...

I discerned a multitude of faces

Overlooking, yesterday, feathers on the shoulders

Long necklaces, going up Sainte-Catherine

In the hope of being entertained, of loving, bare back

Made up in common, I put on a t-shirt...

We listened to Radio Vitamine, before going out...

There were deserted beaches, I remember...

Philosopher, Baroque convoy, Bohemian troops

Around a castle, definitive rejoicing...

Energy demands, again

The will, the trace of words

We drive back to the ports...

Always, grateful

Wandering is vivid, sometimes

We cross these inscriptions

Strange sky of forces...

Parallel to dimensions.

Subjective, led by groups...

Appearances, by clans or squares...

Encrypted voices, slowly, singular idea

From the paths, I walked in the corridors

A square hardly saw us...

And other romantic islands were leaving.

I remembered a speed, words...

Whispered, as soon as dusk, facades

Architectural projection, red ceilings

Or coral, high transparencies...

Automatic, beyond the breathtaking view...

In her direction, drums and acidulous tones

She was titillating a screen...

Restful, with hope erected...

On the surface, chandeliers before

I was so different...

Retrofuturistic visions, there was a reality

Next to the scenery heard, the habits...

Clear of the mutants, an entrance, yesterday...

It takes over the intermediate versions

Universes, a question of perception, strings

By nature, yorkshire-terriers, in the evening, taxis

Yellows, walking under the sky

Purple, drizzle, excess

Squarely on the edge

An R5 was spinning on the road

A long time ago, I was reading

And bouquets of flowers

I told them the colors

I was going backwards

In the bluish spheres

Thrilling moment, at the post office

From the Louvre, to leave...

To I don't know what whole world...

And perfect in our eyes the essential ...

These ideas, these promises, this quest...

Of a happiness, the adventure, the perspectives.

Sometimes the lights sweep the ceiling

An agreement and trees, branches...

Her evasions captivate the gardens...

Green, my summers of yesteryear, roses

On the tablet, no longer faded...

Many years, bohemian moments...

By the way, Hindu tunes, crossovers

Place Blanche, kites taken away...

Hidden fortress

In a village...

From the Languedoc...

The years passed

Swarming, we read

In this world, you have to believe...

In the light, at night...

When discussing the hours.

Representatives of arenas and circles, vast space...

Things continue, driven by the eternal return...

From a link, caresses triumphs, from a few pages

Dehorned, already, by previous readers

As far as the eye can see, tidy books, bohemians...

Blurred images of my light memory...

Animal teams...

Sometimes vegetable...

Mountain, bushy woods.

Ideal image of memories...
Typical, car radio...
I saw my Roman nights again...
Senseless, going to Barcelona

With the stealthy noise of kingdoms on the run
It was a meditative, splendid time...
Memories of trips, expectation of the anchor...
From a link, while we are juxtaposition

From definitive choices, the air of the sea comes to me
Enthusiasm, virgin moment, reachable, rhythm
Fragile, of a universal regime, creates the unforgettable
Passion, as we dreamed, with plans.

The hectic stirrings

On the slice of magazines

Stacked, cross memory

From their foreheads, hours pass

I wasn't imitating anyone

The wind, the purple sky

Quick street tours

Glare...

Delights, after nights...

We accepted everything...

And this chance would mean travel

I put on a t-shirt, then a polo shirt

And there was music...

All day, magnetizations

We were driving towards the coast...

Absolute innocence, illusions.

The emeralds of the gardens, the codes of reality...

Build cobblestones of letters, as in the past...

Castles, guidelines, like a youth

Eternal, curves that bring

Their primordial drunkenness, things

Thus modelable, string theory

Routes, panoramas...

The future, this time...

Her thoughts in lettering.

A long time ago...

We could hear Eagles...

We could hear Rainbow...

We superimposed the clothes

The eras...

The styles...

The places...

So many moments

Successful, cosmopolitan fortune

In the streets of the great century

Inviting, offered themselves to us...

Under a capital vault, there.

They become calmed shores

In our own readings...

As knowledge

Direct access, fluid fabric...

I remembered a room...

Giant, artificial waves

In a cabin in height...

A staircase led to one floor

At dawn, a coffee, at night

Unrest... Ah! we were running...

Imagining other landscapes

After tubular lampshades

Dreams are rushing...

At the wave dizzy

I was hoping for a merger...

Something alchemical.

Together, we write

Climate energy

Casual branches

I extract a culmination...

Experiences, from all sides

In such places, intermittent...

Some summer evenings, in the cellars...

Era of improvisations and mixtures

Festive, young adults of ancient times.

In this story...

There was a little bit of Oxygen...

Of Equinox, rapprochements

Unknown liqueurs, the clear way

And sails, the summer sky...

On the wet sand, antique

Ringing shores, impatience...

Ingénue, automatic crossed

Always go somewhere else...

Each level unleashes its power...

Invisible, under the sheets, under the bases

Summer, at the heart of journeys, stories.

Intoxicating approaches...

Monumental building

Wings, esplanade, tapas

Japanese Bar of the Old

Stadium or Park...

Time releases

Elders, in the South

Before going out again

Then the days passed

In urban alcoves

With the flow of time...

We had that freedom...

Rites, some cyclical universe

Right in the middle of the garden, speed...

Close to that of light...

A moment, unspeakable trances...

I remember an omen

Parallel passions...

There was a shortcut...

For hours, walking...

We finished a bottle...

We assumed, by memory

From causes to consequences...

Behind translucent doors

These years, I had loved them...

And time passed, after a summer...

Hot, I thought of that youth...

Spaces to conquer, in other worlds

On a neighboring planet, civilizations...

At sleepy rays, I had to stroll...

From place to daydreams, indefinable inspiration

Clouds, a force that encrypts, in every plan

Universe as the slightest gesture, after the road

Paper libraries...

Free drift, students...

Designers, silhouettes

Boroughs...

My shady cat's eyes

From a green of possible moments...

Manna-hata, the densest...

In those unlikely moments

Part of mystery...

It was a strange time

Paper-sized...

Largesse, near the driveway

Steep, sumptuous...

In the morning, everything starts again

So many glimmers, consciousness

Filled sequences...

Dress code...

Noise that cups make...

Resting, brief agreements

Illusions, we all crossed paths...

12

I reserved my energy

Under the monumental dome

Exhilarating times...

I read, sometimes, in sweatshirts...

Deus Ex Machina Tokyo Address...

I remember all this, recess

New times

Slopes of ecstasy

From this place...

Spaces, light
Interior, power...
Who tries to make it last...
Days passed, sometimes

Tunnels, trains...
Foundation of the World...
So, between two bays
The canvas took its place

Drunk sheets, I was reading
In the rustic living room
We interfered
Between sequences...

Creatures, reason for seconds...

We were together, a few times...

Together, by June fever, unnoticed

Illuminated ancestry of indirect projectors

Victories, when I was a child...

Already, walking under the purple sky...

The drizzle, it joined the space...

At the foot of Mount Royal, Water Polo

Shortly after the inauguration...

From Space, already drunk to the River

Ink, red or coral ceilings...

Transparencies, mysterious mist

The Square looked like a park

I remembered the thread of the night

Slammed doors, incarnations

In our preparatory thoughts...

13

At the top of a building, overlooking a beach...

Artificial, where unexpected illusions extend

Supremacy, high towers, I listened to the orange beat

Blue, unconditional

Receptacle of Jupiter

This abundant space...

The South, a feverish moment

Baz'Art Café of the nights

Summer, seemed so far away...

Hugely behind

Constellation, the horizon

Became months flown away

It was the Nuit blanche

The century in the bubbles...

A little less behind...

Warmth of the new city...

After seasons, appeasement

I exhaust this world late...

Released, have fun the turret ...

From a castle, to the bottom of a park

One entry, speeds during the summer.

A week before Christmas...

There was entertainment...

Mezzanines, a look at periods

Favorite subjects, cosmos

There was the white night crowd

Youth, great steps, pastille

Nostalgic, tourist compartment

Near a porthole, unreal universe...

Thirsty for emotions...

Printing, advances...

Distracting satisfaction...

There is an invisible foundation

Sometimes structuring cheerfulness

Imperceptibly, tinted

Of cachet, of campaign...

Transformation of hours.

14

Tiny lights

Flickering, scattered

Conquest of a space

Constellation of flowers...

State of mind of the time...

There were thousands of words

In the air, the bastions are reborn...

The splendor would last endlessly, turns ...

Instead, we were giving America.

Immensity, currents or brews...

Who got there, wild coasts...

Distracted, with tranquil landscapes

From a particular resource of truces...

Month, flags, the chapel

Notre-Dame-de-Lourdes...

Coming back, feeling of being...

A real individual from those times

Feeling of adventure, hotel room...

Café, there was a high table made of light wood

I remembered that I had been another

That myself, momentum, azure hourglass...

In time, I remember...

Sometimes my life was different

We stopped the restored car

Afterwards, we drove towards the coast...

Going through the power...

Heterogeneous canvases, crumpled sheets...

I remember one night, that naked troupe...

Under the slide, coming from Amsterdam

Monarchy, buildings

The same sequence...

The idea of a wormhole...

Then belonged to the foam

Pleasure softens...

Great Sarabande...

I was erasing the numbers...

Years, which I replaced.

15

Society of meditative rounds...

Our transmutation was far away

Stones polished in famous speed...

Shoes worthy of ribambelles

Will come from the universes, in the long run

These acres of pure ease...

There was a large courtyard...

Inner, we would create beings

More slender, depending on the location...

From this writing, I read...

There were worlds...

Icy, bluster...

Passages, an entire century

Exotic, floor...

From a building...

Near a property

Protected, orange...

Leaf shovels

Ordinary patina...

The night sparkled...

Like a processor.

In the fog of an era...

Giant lions of the squares, walks...

Floating cities, wooded islands, built

Winds and dust swept the outside

The platform, remember...

Huge gardens, a hundred leagues away

Routines, mesmerizing armada

It was so easy to please us...

Because we wanted it...

I was watering my fate...

Stolen images...

In the deckchairs of the garden

We met again quickly

In Rotterdam, tankers, offshore air

Possible agreements of the road...

Let's go back a moment...

16

I remembered the time...

And worlds, to observe...

I only put on a t-shirt

And at night...

Would we remember...

Two or three sequences

Trees are spying on me...

At the dawn of the crossings

The capitals there...

The day, the strength...

Surrounding words

Metamorphosed...

Especially at that time

At the same time chance, imagination...

The eternity of a few streets...

And there was like a perfume...

From the early eighties

And I was going there in slow motion

By quiet touches

As in a thesis

Magnetic and slow...

Fickle flowerbeds...

Embellished, reliefs

Browsed, seconds

In appearance, beaches

Almost endless...

The music of the gypsies...

Stranded tree trunks...

Sometimes, Les Indes galantes

Millions of years

And by the clans...

Cacti, succulent

The taste of a rhythm

Dreamlike ribbon, cavales

In the background, balance

From sailors, passion...

Slow liners, a thousand years old.

17

Emotion, in our spaces...

Dematerialized, new exaltation

Reopened wider tracks...

Freedom of an era...

Vineyards from other worlds

Other stories, perhaps

Special resource...

Arid happiness, memories...

Dimensional journeys.

Happiness was reality...

That I keep in this chest...

Relieved of the crowd's ambitions

Gathering that sang...

Happiness, radiant becomings...

Comes forward, intrigued, illusions...

Discreet streets, station, glow...

From bikinis, memories of dances

Of emotion, coast of utopias...

Piano of music lovers, sometimes...

On the horizon, giants of the future...

He enjoyed the moment, free suite.

Millennium erected...

On bitter answers

It really existed

During these readings...

Of these approvals...

I know nomads...

With the sea as a destiny

Omen of a new page

Honey, licorice, money changers...

She was scrolling through the images...

Ultra-perfect versions of models

Originals, with magical sanctuaries

Lapses, and I was reading...

Accumulation of works...

He's a spacer A star chaser...

Perhaps it is futile to understand.

18

And really, the time of the crowds

Ignoring routine, on the street...

Escapes from an illusion...

The world had been a feast

Then it became advanced

Like a perfume of Forum

In the early eighties

Décor, with bright orange walls...

In the evening, exhilarating jubilation, liberating.

At the turn of the century, worshippers...

Revolve around maps, constantly

This time heads of the pediments after...

At the edge of trophies, ephemeral glory

Virtual aptitude...

To find the beautiful life...

And so was the world

Untied, a few steps away...

Maybe even intended...

To the attraction of the coasts...

And there was music...

All day, in a mall...

Which served as a meeting place

I wanted to spread out my time...

In dreamlike music...

Multicolored sprinter screen

Again, the Moon was coming...

The bluish black was offered to me

After the laughing balancing...

Limits of the ordinary, summer...

Like that, under a dome...

Perhaps, the hours were stopping...

Full of elixir, there were streets...

Transverse, small streets...

Human...

Between plants

Truces...

A long story...

19

I remembered a speed, words

Squarely on the edge

To I don't know what whole world...

Place Blanche, kites taken away...

Mountain, bushy woods...

From a link, while we are juxtaposition

Glare...

Routes, panoramas

So many moments...

A staircase led to one floor...

Era of improvisations and mixtures

Always go somewhere else...

Before going out again...

These years, I had loved them...

Universe as the slightest gesture, after the road

Steep, sumptuous...

Slopes of ecstasy...

The canvas took its place...

I remembered the thread of the night

Baz'Art Café of the nights...

The century in the bubbles...

Near a porthole, unreal universe...

The splendor would last endlessly, turns ...

Feeling adventurous, hotel room

I remember one night, that naked troupe

There was a large courtyard...

Protected, orange...

It was so easy to please us

At the dawn of the crossings...

And there was like a perfume...

Sometimes, Les Indes galantes...

Arid happiness, memories...

From bikinis, memories of dances

Omen of a new page...

In the evening, exhilarating jubilation, liberating

And so was the world...

Limits of the ordinary, summer...

© KDP Editions (Seatle, Washington, United States) 2022
ISBN : 9798843839901 (Printed book)
Standard Copyright License